Cell Phones and S

D0431689

Cell Phones: Threats to Privacy and Security

Other titles in the *Cell Phones and Society* series include:

Cell Phones and Society

Cell Phones:
Threats to Privacy
and Security

Patricia D. Netzley

ReferencePoint
Press®

San Diego, CA

For more information, contact:
ReferencePoint Press, Inc.
PO Box 27779
San Diego, CA 92198
www.ReferencePointPress.com

LIBRARY OF CONGRESS CATALOGING-IN-PUBLICATION DATA

Netzley, Patricia D.
  Cell phones: threats to privacy and security / by Patricia D. Netzley.
    pages cm. — (Cell phones and society)
  Audience: Grade 9 to 12.
  Includes bibliographical references and index.
  ISBN-13: 978-1-60152-668-7 (hardback)
  ISBN-10: 1-60152-668-7 (hardback)
  1. Cell phones and teenagers—Juvenile literature. 2. Cell phones—Security measures—Juvenile literature. I. Title.
  HQ799.2.C45N48 2014
  303.48'30835--dc23
                                                          2014008036

Contents

Benefits Versus Risks

Cell phones have provided society with many benefits. Their portability enables users to talk to friends or call for help from anywhere there is a communication system capable of connecting one phone to another. A type of cell phone called a smartphone also allows individuals to access the Internet while mobile, making business transactions and online entertainment activities just as easy to conduct while traveling as at home. But there are downsides to cell phones as well. All kinds of cell phones can make users vulnerable to invasions of privacy, and smartphones can also expose them to serious financial security threats.

Open to Thieves

Security experts warn that smartphones are never 100 percent private. *Consumer Reports* magazine explains: "When you take your phone into your confidence, so to speak, you're also taking in a host of parties that make all of those wonderful mobile services possible, including app developers, your wireless carrier and phone manufacturer, mobile advertisers, and the maker of your phone's operating system."[1] All of these entities can collect data, such as a phone's location or unique ID, that allow the user's online and physical movements to be tracked.

Thieves can use apps to access phone data as well, typically to steal personal information related to financial transactions. A study by *Consumer Reports* suggests that in 2013 roughly 1.6 million smartphone users were tricked into installing a malicious app—made to look like a legitimate one—that allowed a thief to intercept credit card information during online transactions and/or steal banking passwords or other sensitive information. Thieves can also install harmful software in a phone by sending an e-mail or message that tricks a phone user into visiting a malicious website and unknowingly downloading the software.

In addition, security experts warn that smartphones can be hacked (accessed by someone without authorization to do so) just as a computer can. This is because whenever a smartphone is on, it is usually connected to the Internet. Moreover, as cybersecurity expert John Hale notes, "Your cell phone really is a small computer."[2]

Millions of Users

No one knows just how many people have had their cell phones hacked. However, the number of potential victims is growing because of the rise in smartphone use. *Consumer Reports* estimates that in 2013 more than half of all American adults used such a device, and more than 100 million relied on their smartphone to conduct business transactions using either the Internet or an app. However, security experts say that there are ways to protect a phone from invasion by thieves. These include installing apps cautiously and not accessing the Internet via unsecure wi-fi connections, such as ones provided at hotels and airports. In regard to the latter, David Jacobs of the Electronic Privacy Information Center, a consumer advocacy group, says, "Most consumers don't realize when they're transmitting info over an open Wi-Fi network that it can be intercepted."[3]

> "Your cell phone really is a small computer."[2]
>
> —Cybersecurity expert John Hale.

Security experts add that it is important to have safety features on a phone in case the device is stolen. Without these, thieves can easily access the phone's personal data. One such security measure is a screen lock with a strong password that blocks anyone without the password from using the phone. Another is an app that allows the phone's owner to erase all of its data from a remote location upon realizing the phone has been lost or stolen. Although smartphone users are typically connected to the Internet for long periods, experts say that taking such precautions can make smartphones as safe as home computers.

Tracking Features

Experts also say that people who want to keep themselves safe and protect their privacy need to educate themselves on how phones and apps work. Many phone users install apps without any consideration of security issues. Yet studies have shown that approximately one out of three apps requires the user to provide permission for the app to access personal data, such as contact lists, that the app does not actually need in order to function properly. This makes that data needlessly vulnerable.

"Most consumers don't realize when they're transmitting info over an open Wi-Fi network that it can be intercepted."[3]

—David Jacobs of the Electronic Privacy Information Center.

In addition, all smartphones have a feature known as location tracking that can be both helpful and harmful. This feature makes it possible to learn the location of a phone if it has been lost or stolen and allows apps to base information on a user's location. For example, the feature allows map apps and real estate apps to provide information based on the user's current location unless the user requests otherwise. But location tracking has also allowed stalkers to find and harm victims who did not know how to turn off the feature.

Surveillance

Many phone users are also unaware of the degree to which law enforcement agencies and other government entities can intercept communications and access their phone records—the logs of what numbers were called, when they were called, and how long the conversations lasted. This is the case with both smartphones and regular cell phones. All phones are vulnerable to wiretapping, a form of real-time electronic eavesdropping that allows police to listen in on conversations with a court's permission. (The word *wiretapping* refers to the fact that noncellular phones rely on a system of wires to communicate; tapping into—or connecting a listening device to—these wires provides access to any conversations made on a particular phone line.)

In addition, because of laws passed to combat terrorism after the attacks of September 11, 2001, law enforcement officials who have

Smartphones benefit users of all ages, but privacy and security vulnerabilities are a growing concern. Tracking features, malicious apps, and hacking all pose threats to users.

a court order to do so can monitor any phone a suspected criminal might have access to, not only phones ordinarily used by the suspect. This means that if a suspected terrorist visits the home of an innocent person, the phone in that home might be subjected to a wiretap. The 9/11 attacks also triggered the creation of a classified government surveillance program whereby certain kinds of information can be gathered without first getting a court order. As details about this program have leaked out, many Americans have become concerned about the privacy of their cell phone conversations.

Security experts counter that since most law-abiding Americans are unlikely to be the target of a government wiretap, the greater concern should be the risk that criminals, friends, or relatives might compromise cell phone security or privacy. New technologies are making wiretapping so easy that a jealous boyfriend, for example, can eavesdrop on his girlfriend's phone conversations without being detected. It is also fairly easy for someone who steals a phone to access its stored personal data unless its owner has taken measures to prevent this. Such preventions and other safety measures greatly reduce the risks related to cell phone use. Therefore, technology experts argue, there is no need to be afraid to use a cell phone, just a need to be cautious while using one.

Keeping Conversations Private

Chapter One

In September 2013 the director general of the US National Security Agency (NSA) testified before a congressional committee about privacy abuses related to phone use. He revealed that while gathering information related to the phone calls of suspected terrorists, some NSA employees eavesdropped on the conversations of their boyfriends, girlfriends, or spouses. The media dubbed this illegal activity *loveint*, for "love intelligence"—collecting intelligence (spying) on loved ones.

There were approximately a dozen such cases of abuse of power from 2003 to 2013. One case, however, involved a woman who might have begun listening in on conversations as far back as 1998 and continued doing so for five years. In other cases, the NSA workers' efforts to listen in on conversations were unsuccessful, so they could access nothing but phone records. Known as metadata, these records provide information on who was called, when each call was placed, how long each call lasted, and the name, address, and account information of the phone's owner. Still, the NSA's employees were supposed to examine metadata associated only with possible terrorism cases.

Privacy and Surveillance Laws

The news that government employees have been spying on private citizens who have no connections to terrorism outraged many people. Shortly after the abuses came to light, Anthony Romero, executive director of the American Civil Liberties Union (ACLU), complained, "What's clear about the instances of abuse is that these have nothing to do with terrorism. This is about individuals prying into the private lives of the people closest to them. It's an abuse of government data that should not be in the government's hands."[4]

Listening in on cell phone conversations for personal reasons is illegal in the United States under the Electronic Communications

Privacy Act. This law makes it a federal crime to wiretap someone without court approval unless one of the participants in the call has given permission for the wiretap. (However, some state laws mandate that both parties must consent to a call's being recorded in order for the recording to be legal.) It is also a federal crime to reveal the information gathered via an illegal wiretap to anyone else or to use it for personal or professional gain.

Law enforcement officials are allowed to wiretap, but typically this occurs only if they can show probable cause that the wiretap will support suspicions that the person being tapped is involved in unlawful activity. The unlawful activity must be one of a small number of certain crimes, as defined by the law of the state in which the law enforcement operation is taking place. In California, for example, wiretaps are allowed only for a limited number of serious felonies, including murder, acts of terrorism, and kidnapping for ransom or extortion. In explaining such limits, the Shouse California Law Group says,

> If the police have reason to believe that a major bank robbery is about to take place, and a wiretap of a certain phone would almost certainly give them the evidence they need to arrest the ringleader and stop the robbery ... they still will not be able to get an order [from a court] authorizing the wiretap, because robbery is not one of the specified crimes.[5]

If the right criteria have been met, however, a judge will provide law enforcement officers with a court order to wiretap. A type of search warrant, this order typically limits the period that the wiretapping may take place and mandates that it concern only conversations related to the suspected illegal activity.

In 2002, however, in an effort to prevent further acts of terrorism like those of 9/11, President George W. Bush signed a secret executive order allowing the NSA to listen in on Americans' phone conversations without first obtaining a warrant. The existence of this order was leaked in 2005, and the following year the American public learned that Bush had also created the NSA's metadata collection program. In

At a 2006 Arizona rally demonstrators protest government wiretapping and surveillance. The American public learned that year of a secret presidential order allowing the National Security Agency to listen in on phone conversations without a warrant.

addition to phone records, this collection includes text messages and e-mails that travel from a computer or smartphone to their intended recipients via telecommunications companies' wires and fiber optic networks.

Minimal Intrusion?

The NSA says that its agents do not read each text message and e-mail. Instead, these communications are subjected to a data mine, a type of data processing that looks for terrorism-related keywords. If these words are found in a message, then that message is examined further to determine whether people are indeed communicating about terrorist activities. The NSA also says that most of its Internet data collecting focuses on individuals living outside of the United States, but critics of the agency doubt this is true. Similarly, the NSA asserts that its stored phone records are in the form of bulk data, and individual records are examined only if they are later discovered to have a link to a terrorism threat—in which case, the agency says, it gets a court order before delving deeper into the circumstances of the phone call.

The collection of this data is authorized under section 215 of the USA Patriot Act, an antiterrorism law that requires any person or entity to turn over information that might protect the United States against terrorist attacks. Telecommunications companies are therefore legally compelled to turn over the requested metadata. They are also required, based on a 1994 law called the Digital Telephony Act, to make all digital communications—which include text messages as well as any voice communications transmitted digitally—available to law enforcement officials in the same way they make traditional voice transmissions available.

However, Mark Klein, who worked as a technician with the telecommunications company AT&T for twenty-two years, claims that to make the process of gathering data even easier, the government has installed devices at many of the main junction points in the US telecommunications system. These allow the government direct access to the data. Specifically, the devices make copies of the data passing through them, including text messages and e-mails, and send one of these data streams directly to a government location for storage and analysis.

Collecting Conversations?

Experts disagree on whether the NSA's metadata program is a necessary tool in the war on terrorism. The NSA reports that in October 2013 the program stopped fifty-four terrorist attacks, but a subsequent study by a White House review board found that the information that prevented terrorist attacks could have been gathered through other means. In either case, it does appear that the data can provide vital information to aid an investigation of an attack that has already taken place. As an example, experts cite the case of the terrorist bombing that occurred during the Boston Marathon in 2013. According to anonymous government sources, federal investigators studied both pre- and post-bombing phone records to see how often Katherine Russell, the widow of one of the suspected bombers, had been in contact with the suspects. In this way they hoped to determine whether she had been involved in the plot.

However, during an interview with CNN reporter Erin Burnett about the Boston bombing case, former FBI counterterrorism expert Tim Clemente revealed that the investigators might have access to recordings of Russell's actual phone conversations as well, some dating back to before they suspected she was associated with terrorism.

Emergency personnel assist people injured by a bomb explosion at the finish line of the 2013 Boston Marathon. Federal investigators obtained important information by searching phone records in connection with the suspected bombers.

Specifically, Clemente suggested that the NSA has been automatically recording and storing everyone's phone conversations for years. He told Burnett,

> We certainly have ways in national security investigations to find out exactly what was said in that conversation [between Russell and her husband]. It's not necessarily something that the FBI is going to want to present in court, but it may help lead the investigation and/or lead to questioning of her. All that stuff [said on the phone] is being captured as we speak whether we know it or like it or not.[6]

Glenn Greenwald, a columnist for the British newspaper the *Guardian*, says that this revelation supports a claim made by the *Washington Post* in 2010 that the NSA collects and stores 1.7 billion e-mails, phone calls, and other digital communications daily—that is, not just metadata but actual conversations. He accuses the United States of being "a ubiquitous, limitless Surveillance State"[7] whose citizens cannot expect that any of their digital communications are private. But whether or not this is true, the ACLU, which fights to protect people's constitutional rights, notes that even the perception that it is true can have a "chilling effect on public discourse." The group explains: "If people think that their conversations and their e-mails [or] their reading habits are being monitored, people will inevitably feel less comfortable saying what they think, especially if what they think is not what the government wants them to think."[8]

Defenders of the NSA, however, argue that thinking the government would want to record every person's phone calls every day is an example of paranoia—an unreasonable belief that someone is spying on you, following you, plotting ways to hurt you, or otherwise trying to harm you. People involved in the NSA program insist that the agency is not routinely recording, storing, and/or listening to ordinary

> "All that stuff [said on the phone] is being captured as we speak whether we know it or like it or not."[6]
>
> —Former FBI counterterrorism expert Tim Clemente.

Wiretap Payments

In 2012 the cell phone industry disclosed that it was profiting from wiretapping. For example, AT&T charged $325 to wiretap a phone—a cost it called an activation fee—and $10 for each day the wiretap was kept in place. Verizon charged the government $775 for the first month of a wiretap and $500 for every month thereafter. People disagree on whether this practice is a good thing. Some say that it is a bad idea for phone companies to turn spying on phone users into a highly profitable business. Others say that if wiretapping were free, then it would be used indiscriminately, and at least the billing process creates records that others can use to make sure wiretaps are not abused. Meanwhile, cellular companies insist that they are not overcharging because there is a lot of work involved in wiretapping, and most companies charge nothing when the wiretap is associated with an emergency situation like a missing child.

Americans' phone conversations, and they point out that the illegal activities of their employees who listened in on calls was dealt with swiftly and harshly. Moreover, in response to criticism of the NSA's efforts, US president Barack Obama has stated, "I am comfortable that the program currently is not being abused. I am comfortable that if the American people examined exactly what was taking place, how it was being used, what the safeguards were, that they would say, 'You know what? These folks are following the law.'"[9]

NSA Reforms

Nonetheless, in January 2014 President Obama announced that he would be making changes to some aspects of the NSA surveillance program. While metadata would still be collected and evaluated, the people assigned to study collected data would be required to limit their examinations to communications no more than two steps away from the suspected terrorist or organization. In other words, only people in close contact with the suspect would have their phone records examined. In addition, the NSA would be required to get approval from a special judge before examining a person's data.

Obama also said that his staff would be looking into other restrictions and safeguards designed to protect Americans' right to privacy, and some of these restrictions and safeguards would be extended to foreigners as well. The attorney general and the director of national intelligence would also be seeking a new location for metadata storage in order to greatly restrict access to this material and prevent abuses. Obama also called on the members of Congress to address concerns regarding privacy and civil liberty issues by making necessary changes to the Patriot Act.

Listening Devices

Issues related to the NSA's surveillance activities have received a great deal of attention in the media. But experts say that at least as much concern should be paid to how easy it can be for ordinary people to listen in on seemingly private conversations. As the Privacy Rights Clearing House, an organization that educates the public on privacy issues, reports, "The determined eavesdropper will find a variety of sophisticated electronic surveillance and listening devices on the market."[10]

> "The determined eavesdropper will find a variety of sophisticated electronic surveillance and listening devices on the market."[10]
>
> —Privacy Rights Clearing House, a nonprofit group dedicated to protecting people's privacy.

One type of listening device is the roving bug, a piece of software that can be installed on a cell phone to remotely activate its microphone. When this technology first appeared in the early 2000s, it was installed either by someone with physical access to the phone or remotely by a phone company, typically at the request of a law enforcement officer armed with a warrant. Now, however, hackers—people who use computers to gain unauthorized access to data—have discovered how to install microphone-activating software remotely. It allows the microphone to be turned on even when the phone is not being used to make a call, and any conversations or other sounds in the vicinity of the phone are then transmitted to the eavesdropper. A similar recording device works with a cell phone's Bluetooth headset to transmit sounds

One type of listening device works with Bluetooth headsets. However, this device cannot be installed remotely by, for example, a hacker.

through the headset's earpiece. However, this device can be installed only by someone with physical access to the headset.

Using a listening device is not the same as performing a wiretap. As the Shouse California Law Group explains, "Eavesdropping and wiretapping are similar but they're not the same. Basically, the difference is that wiretapping is the act of intercepting and listening in on conversations by tapping into the phone line . . . while eavesdropping is the act of listening in on conversations using an electronic device but without tapping a phone line."[11] As an example, the law group says that if a business owner sets up microphones to secretly record the phone conversations of employees to find out whether they are trying to steal money from him, he would be guilty of eavesdropping, not wiretapping.

Spying on World Leaders

In 2013 a former employee of the NSA, Edward Snowden, leaked classified documents related to NSA surveillance activities. Among these documents was proof that the US government had been monitoring the phone conversations of thirty-five world leaders, allies as well as enemies. The allies were outraged over the breach of trust. For example, German chancellor Angela Merkel said, "Spying between friends, that's just not done." In her country, the newspaper *Der Spiegel* investigated the situation and found that American intelligence officers had been using the US embassy in Berlin as a base from which to use sophisticated interception technology to eavesdrop on Merkel's cell phone. The United States denied that it was currently eavesdropping on Merkel—although the government neither denied nor admitted having spied on her in the past. In January 2014, however, US president Barack Obama ordered the NSA to stop spying on world leaders. The following month the German newspaper *Bild am Sonntag* reported that an anonymous NSA employee had told the paper that although the United States was no longer spying on Merkel, it was continuing to spy on her aides as well as more than three hundred German politicians.

Quoted in *Spiegel* Staff, "Embassy Espionage: The NSA's Secret Spy Hub in Berlin," *Spiegel* Online, October 27, 2013. www.spiegel.de.

Twelve US states require everyone involved in a conversation to agree to its recording in order for the recording to be legal. Thirty-eight states say that such a recording is legal if only one party has given consent for the recording. Federal law also requires the consent of one party. The Digital Media Law Project, which educates people on legal issues related to digital technology, says that such consent is critical to avoid prosecution, adding that

> regardless of whether state or federal law governs the situation, it is almost always illegal to record a phone call or private conversation to which you are not a party, do not have consent from at least one party, and could not natural-

ly overhear. In addition, federal and many state laws do not permit you to surreptitiously place a bug or recording device on a person or telephone, in a home, office or restaurant to secretly record a conversation between two people who have not consented.[12]

Intercepting Conversations

It is also illegal to secretly record conversations via a video camera. Nonetheless, some people use apps that can remotely activate a cell phone's camera and audio feed in order to record both sounds and images. There are many online articles that can guide people in how to turn a cell phone into a spy camera. As Joshua Sherman of *Digital Trends* magazine notes, in most cases "getting and installing the software on your smartphone is easy." He adds, "We're in the second decade of the 21st century. You don't need to buy a bunch of expensive equipment to spy anymore. These days, all you need is an old smartphone."[13] Experts say that professional spies also employ cell phone cameras for espionage, but they typically swap their target's cell phone with a seemingly identical one that has been modified so that the spy can activate the microphone and camera at will and access text messages and other information from the phone.

Another way to gain access to text messages is via a cell phone's subscriber identity module (SIM) card, a smart card that is unique to its owner and stores the phone's personal data. Although the phone will not work without it, the card is removable. If it is placed in a device known as a spy SIM card reader and that reader is inserted into the USB port of a computer, the computer can read all of the phone's text messages, even ones that the phone's user deleted. The SIM reader is easy to use and easy to purchase online. Also easy to use are devices that can record the numbers a phone is calling and/or the

> "Regardless of whether state or federal law governs the situation, it is almost always illegal to record a phone call or private conversation to which you are not a party, do not have consent from at least one party, and could not naturally overhear."[12]
>
> —*The Digital Media Law Project provides advice and information on media-related laws.*

numbers of the calls being received by the phone. However, it is illegal to put these or any other spying devices on a phone without the owner's knowledge.

Hackers can also intercept text messages, instant messages, and digital photos as this data is transmitted from a cell phone to the tele-communications company's cell tower or base station. Mobile phone applications encrypt this data, but most hackers can decrypt it. Most are also skilled enough to adapt to each advance in cell phone security in order to continue their snooping.

Spyware

In addition, hackers continually work to place spying software, known as spyware or snoopware, into people's phones. One way is by tricking phone users into clicking on a link that will infect the phone with the spyware. Hackers can also install spyware on a phone when it is using a free, unsecured wireless connection.

> "Any person's cell phone can be used as a remote listening device that will spy on its owner."[14]
>
> —The website for the mSpy app.

Easy-to-install apps allow nonhackers to spy on a cell phone user as well, providing the snoop can sneak the app onto the phone without the user's knowledge. Once installed, these apps are invisible to the user as they constantly monitor calls, text messages, and the phone's location. The promotional video for one such app, mSpy, outlines its benefits: "Any person's cell phone can be used as a remote listening device that will spy on its owner. Personal conversations, business meetings, everything they don't want you to hear will be recorded for you to listen to."[14]

Use Increasing

Experts say that despite the fact that spying on someone via intrusive software on the victim's cell phone is illegal, the activity is increasing. The most common purpose of this spying is to find out whether a boyfriend, girlfriend, or spouse is cheating on the person doing the spying. Private investigators who work to uncover cheaters say that they turn away people who want them to use unlawful spyware. One such investigator, Adam Virzi, says,

There are definitely lawful ways to get this information [if you suspect your partner is cheating]. It usually involves surveillance of the subject and documents their activities during times when the person is likely to be going to see somebody else. It's a long way around it when you think about spying devices, but it's also the lawful way of doing it.[15]

The companies that provide spy technology, however, do not see anything wrong with it. One such company that provides cell phone spying services insists, "If you have a committed relationship with your partner or are responsible for a child or employee, you have a right to know. To protect your relationship, spy on their mobile phone."[16]

For a yearly fee, this company makes it possible for its clients to listen to mobile phone calls live, turn the mobile microphone and camera on at will, view all photos on the phone, read all messages on the phone, and view the phone user's website history, address book, and calendars. The company addresses legal issues by saying that the software required for its services "is perfectly legal to install on your own phone. . . . But please make sure you have explicit permission from the person whose phone you will be monitoring and whose phone you will require physically in order to physically install [our software] on to it before proceeding any further."[17] However, there is no way to verify whether the person using the phone will really know that such monitoring is going on since this type of spying is undetectable.

In fact, spying via cell phone has become so hard to detect that experts warn cell phone users never to leave their phones unattended lest someone install spyware on the phone. Experts also warn cell phone users not to download apps or other data from unknown sources and to avoid visiting unreliable websites or clicking on suspicious links. But even with these precautions, there is still the risk that conversations or messages will be overheard or intercepted, and it is also possible that phone records will end up in the wrong hands. Therefore, some experts say that the only way to ensure that private conversations will remain private is not to use a cell phone at all—an unlikely choice in a world where cell phones have become such an integral part of daily life.

Is Someone Tracking Your Movements?

After reading about cell phone security issues, science writer Ben Goldacre decided to try an experiment. He wanted to find out whether he could use his live-in girlfriend's cell phone to stalk her. He started by registering her phone on a website that tracks movements for a fee. He needed her phone to be able to do this, so he waited until she was out of the house and had left the phone behind. Immediately after he keyed in the information, her phone received a text message saying that Goldacre was requesting that she add him to her list of friends. To do this, all Goldacre needed to do was reply to the message with a text message saying simply "LOCATE." Once he did this, the phone received a text message stating that other people would now be able to keep track of the phone's location. Goldacre deleted this message and the previous one; no more messages were sent after that.

From that point on, Goldacre could go to the company's website and view a map showing the exact location of the phone. About how easy this was, Goldacre says, "There is no trace of what I'm doing on her phone. I can't quite believe my eyes; I knew that the police could do this, and telecommunications companies, but not any old random person with five minutes access to someone else's phone. . . . As devious systems go, it's foolproof."[18] Goldacre also reports that the website had settings allowing him to receive notifications of her location at regular intervals. In addition, it could provide him with a map of her route and make the phone's camera secretly take a picture of its surroundings every half hour.

Basic Technology

The ability to track phones in this way has existed for years; Goldacre's experiment took place in 2006. One reason is that cell phone technology makes the devices relatively easy to track. Cell phones work like two-way radios, sending and receiving radio signals from the cell phone towers and base stations that make up the cellular communications system. As the person using the phone travels from place to place with the device, a signal being sent to or from a particular tower or base station gets stronger or weaker depending on how close or how far away the phone is from the tower or base. When the signal gets too weak for a particular base station to handle, the cellular system transfers the signal to the next base station in the series of cells that make up the system.

Matthew Blaze, a professor of computer and information science at the University of Pennsylvania, explains: "At any given instant, a cell company has to know where you are; it is constantly registering with the tower with the strongest signal."[19] In fact, in order to maintain a strong signal, a cell company can register the location of a particular cell phone as often as every seven seconds. But even when an exact location is not available, computers can use the strength of a signal, the amount of time it takes the signal to travel from point to point along the system, and the angle of a signal's approach to various cell towers to determine where a phone is located.

Another way to determine where a phone is located is via a GPS receiver. *GPS* stands for "global positioning system," a system of satellites orbiting Earth. This system was established by the US military, but the government allows others to use it as well. A GPS receiver uses the system by locating four or more satellites, determining how far it is away from each one, and then using this information to figure out its own location. To find a satellite, the receiver analyzes the radio signals emitted by the satellites, timing how long it takes for them to travel to Earth. This is a complicated process because of the way satellites transmit and the various factors in space that can influence the transmission. Ultimately, however, the receiver can calculate its own position with a great degree of accuracy. Most GPS receivers can also show their own location on a map, chart their path on that map, and determine the speed at which they are moving.

Modern smartphones, with GPS capabilities, can fairly accurately calculate their position on a map. While this has many benefits, it can also allow others to track the user's movements.

A Beneficial Service

Almost all phones can be located through one method or another, although smartphones are easier to locate than traditional cell phones. As long as a smartphone is turned on, it constantly sends information to cell phone towers even when it is not being used, whereas traditional cell phones send signals only when calls are made. There are also many location-sharing smartphone apps that people can use to share their location with their friends, and smartphones offer a find-your-phone feature as well. This allows someone with a lost phone to use a website to locate their own phone. However, smartphones do offer users the option of turning off this feature as well as blocking apps from using the tracking feature.

In addition, the method of using cell phone tower and base station information to track a phone typically requires the cooperation of communications companies. Many tracking services are able to obtain this cooperation. An example is Life360.com, a free service created to help find missing children or confused adults who have become lost. Using cell phone towers from wireless carriers like T-Mobile and Sprint, the service's website can find a smartphone's location just a few seconds after someone types in its phone number. However, as with the service Goldacre used, the phone's owner must first agree to allow the service by responding to a text message. Dawn Benton, a spokesperson for the wireless carrier company AT&T, says that permission is always required whenever a communications company is involved in a location-tracking service—but as Goldacre proved, it is hard to tell whether the phone's owner is actually the one consenting.

Stalkers

Goldacre tracked his girlfriend for a full week before ending his experiment. During this time he knew where she was, to within 150 yards (137 m) of her location, any time she had her phone with her and turned on. Before his tracking began, he confessed to her about his experiment and she gave permission for it to continue. Had he not offered this information, however, she would not have known that she was being tracked.

Because of this, the Family Abuse Center of Texas (www.family abusecenter.org) has Goldacre's story posted on its website as a way to warn people with abusive partners to be careful about leaving their phones unattended, even for just five minutes, and to leave their phones turned off when they are not making a call. Other abuse centers offer the same kinds of warnings, and some even provide free phones that abuse victims can keep hidden from their partners and use in secret.

Without taking such precautions, people can suffer greatly. "Susan," a woman who has adopted a pseudonym because she is in hiding from an abusive ex-boyfriend, says that before she realized her cell phone was being tracked, she could not figure out how he always knew where she was. She would go on a date with someone else, for example, and afterward he would text her asking how her date had gone, and from his comments it was clear that he knew exactly where she had gone and what she had said while there. She says, "I thought I was going crazy. It's just unnerving knowing that somebody 24/7 knows where you're at, what you're talking about, what's going on, everything about you."[20]

> "It's just unnerving knowing that somebody 24/7 knows where you're at, what you're talking about, what's going on, everything about you."[20]
>
> —"Susan," a woman whose ex-boyfriend was stalking her using a cell phone.

Susan changed her phone number several times in attempt to prevent her ex-boyfriend from contacting her. Nonetheless, because it was her phone and not its number that was enabling the tracking, this failed to end her troubles. She says, "I'd go and change my number at the cell phone store, and he would be calling me on my way home on my new cell phone number."[21] When he started showing up at various places to threaten her, the police served him with a protection order that required him to stay away from her, and Susan went to live in a hotel room. After he showed up there he was arrested for violating the protection order. Finally, after three years of suffering, Susan discovered that her ex-boyfriend had not only been tracking her via her phone but also activating the microphone on her phone without her knowledge.

Damage to Victims

Security expert Robert Siciliano says this is a common aspect of cell phone stalking, along with even more invasive behavior. He reports that in some of the worst cases, "your phone could be sitting next to

Latitude

In February 2009 an add-on to Google Maps was introduced that enabled mobile phone users to view their own locations on a map and share their locations with one another. Called Latitude, it let users control how much they wanted others to see. They could show their exact location, for example, or simply the city where they were located, and they could also turn the feature on or off. From the day Latitude was introduced, privacy- and security-conscious groups were extremely concerned about this add-on. Privacy International said it "could be a gift to stalkers, prying employers, jealous partners, and obsessive friends." This group suggested that hackers might discover how to enable Latitude remotely, someone might receive a Latitude-enabled cell phone as a gift without realizing the feature was turned on, or a stranger in a bar or an abusive spouse might take someone's phone without his or her knowledge and turn on the feature. Google countered that it had built many privacy and safety features into Latitude and was working on making it so all cell phones would alert users whenever Latitude was turned on. The company had already developed this feature for certain types of phones. Nonetheless, fears related to Latitude's safety did not abate, and in August 2013 Google retired the feature.

Quoted in Thomas Claburn, "Google Latitude Spurs Privacy Backlash," Information Week, February 5, 2009. www.informationweek.com.

you while you are watching TV, and somebody can actually log into your phone and can actually watch what you are watching on television."[22] Such behavior can cause great psychological trauma for victims. As Susan says, "You're never the same after this. I think you become a lot more aware of your surroundings, you're not as trusting. You just make it day to day and keep living."[23]

Experts in stalking and similar behaviors say that it is wrong for companies to provide software, apps, and services that make it easier to harass people. Beth Hassett, the executive director of a group that

Stories have been posted online of stalkers following a person's movements with the help of cell phones. In one case, a stalker even activated the phone's microphone without the victim's knowledge.

helps victims of domestic violence, says, "I think it's terrible there are people out there thinking up ways to help people who are engaging in illegal activities do a better job of it."[24] She advocates the creation of laws that will hold companies that make such tools civilly liable for a victim's damages if they cannot prove that a phone's owner gave permission to have their spyware installed on the phone.

Storing Evidence

Some people might wonder why victims like Susan would take so long to figure out that they are being tracked. Experts say that such realizations are often slow to come because few phone users either know about tracking features or understand just how detailed the tracking can be. As Sarah E. Williams, an expert on graphic information, notes, "We are all walking around with little tags, and our tag has a phone number associated with it, who we called and what we do with the phone. We don't even know we are giving up that data."[25]

There have been efforts to educate the public on this subject, not only in the United States but abroad as well. For example, in 2011 Malte Spitz, a privacy advocate and politician in Germany's Green Party, sued his telephone company, Deutsche Telekom, to obtain his phone records and then shared all of this information via a publicly accessible Google document. It showed that over a six-month period the company had identified his exact location (via his longitude and latitude coordinates) more than thirty-five thousand times. Moreover, the company saved this information, so that at any time in the future someone could learn where he had gone each day during the period in question. Spitz finds this particularly disturbing and says, "I want to show the political message that this kind of data retention is really, really big and you can really look into the life of people for six months and see what they are doing where they are."[26]

> "Your phone could be sitting next to you while you are watching TV, and somebody can actually log into your phone and can actually watch what you are watching on television."[22]
>
> —*Security expert Robert Siciliano.*

Subject to Subpoenas

Spitz and others consider the storage of tracking information to be a violation of privacy and a threat to personal security. Law enforcement officials, however, view it as an extremely helpful tool in combating crime. In fact, officials make more than a million requests each year to wireless carriers to turn over user data, which includes text messages and location-tracking information. In most cases these requests are in the form of a subpoena—a written demand to produce evidence—rather than a search warrant or court order, which means that police can make the request without going through a judge. This is all that is required under federal law, which is based on the premise that a phone user has no expectation of privacy in regard to business records kept by a phone company.

Law enforcement officials say that easy access to tracking information improves their chances of catching criminals quickly, thereby increasing public safety. Nonetheless, some state legislators are working to pass laws that make it harder for law enforcement to access phone records. They argue that phone users do have an expectation of privacy when it comes to location data because tracking can reveal personal information related to a person's whereabouts.

Some courts have agreed with this position. For example, in February 2014 the Massachusetts Supreme Judicial Court, the state's highest court, ruled that when people use their cell phones they have a reasonable expectation that this activity will not result in police being able to retrace their steps. In the case before the court, police had used tracking data acquired only while the phone was actively in use, but they did not have a warrant to do this. The majority opinion statement of the court says in part, "Even though restricted to telephone calls sent and received (answered or unanswered), the tracking of the defendant's movements in the urban Boston area for two weeks was more than sufficient to intrude upon the defendant's expectation of privacy."[27]

> "I think it's terrible there are people out there thinking up ways to help people who are engaging in illegal activities do a better job of it."[24]
>
> —Beth Hassett, executive director of a group that helps victims of domestic violence.

New Jersey's highest court came to the same conclusion the previous year, ruling that cell phone location information was protected under a person's constitutional right to privacy. But also that year, the Fifth Circuit US Court of Appeals ruled that police were free to obtain this information without a warrant. In explaining this ruling, the court said, "The caller is not conveying location information to anyone other than his service provider. He is sending information so that the provider can perform the service for which he pays it: to connect his call. And the historical cell site information reveals his location

Stingray Tracking

According to a December 2013 report by *USA Today*, at least twenty-five local and state police departments, as well as the FBI and other federal investigative units, own a Stingray, a mobile device about the size of a suitcase that can function as a cell phone tower. This enables it to receive data from a cell phone just as a real tower would. The device is typically mounted on a surveillance vehicle and driven in areas where law enforcement officers want to gather cell phone data. Officials say they are not listening in on calls but instead are gaining information such as where phones are located, what numbers they have called, and how long these calls lasted. The Stingray allows them to avoid going through a cellular company for this information, and the information is being provided in real time. Some police departments say they use the Stingray only to locate a particular cell phone, such as one belonging to a missing, possibly abducted teenager. But privacy advocacy groups say that the increasing use of the Stingray is disturbing since the mobile device can capture information from all the phones in a given area.

information for addressing purposes, not the contents of his calls."[28] In other words, in the court's view, cell phone location information is different from a private conversation, in that cell phone users willingly provide location information to a company for the purposes of conducting business, much the way addresses are provided to businesses in order to connect people with their mail. That is, in terms of a right to privacy, the court does not equate where someone is located with what someone is saying.

Buying Information

The US Supreme Court has not addressed this issue yet. However, a ruling related to the use of a GPS tracking device has law enforcement agencies concerned about their ability to continue using cell phone tracking. Specifically, the January 2012 ruling found that placing a

GPS tracker on a drug suspect's car was essentially an unreasonable search that violated his or her Fourth Amendment rights. The Fourth Amendment protects people from having their person, possessions, papers, or homes unreasonably searched or seized and requires that any warrants issued for such searches or seizures must be specific and based on probable cause.

Because of such rulings, some state and local law enforcement agencies refuse to rely on tracking information when pursuing suspects, fearing that subsequent arrests or convictions might be challenged. But many agencies do use this information, often paying for it as well. Although federal law requires cell phone companies to turn over information to law enforcement agencies that follow the law in requesting such information, federal law also allows these companies to charge for their cooperation. Many do, charging various prices for different kinds of customer information.

> "We are all walking around with little tags, and our tag has a phone number associated with it, who we called and what we do with the phone. We don't even know we are giving up that data."[25]
>
> —*Sarah E. Williams, an expert on graphic information.*

One type of information is the phone number of every phone that came near a particular cell phone tower during a particular period of time. According to Timothy B. Lee of the technology news website Ars Technica, documents obtained by the ACLU in 2012 "suggest that selling customer information to law enforcement has become a significant revenue source for cell phone companies."[29]

The ACLU documents also show that some law enforcement agencies have decided to engage in cell phone tracking on their own, bypassing the need to contact cell phone companies. For example, the Phoenix suburb of Gilbert, Arizona bought its own cell phone tracking equipment for $244,000. According to ACLU lawyer Catherine Crump, cell phone surveillance has "become run of the mill. And the advances in technology are rapidly outpacing the state of the law."[30]

In addition, perhaps because the law related to tracking is unclear, many law enforcement agencies do not want the public to know just how much they rely on this activity. Eric Lichtblau of the *New York Times*, who studied the ACLU documents, reports that "many [police] departments try to keep cell tracking secret, because of possible backlash from the public and legal problems."[31] As an example of this, the *New York Times* says that the Iowa City Police Department warns its officers not to mention cell phone tracking in police reports. In addition, the department's training manual says, "Do not mention to the public or the media the use of cellphone technology or equipment used to locate the targeted subject."[32]

Monitoring Internet Traffic

The public is also largely unaware of how easy it is for law enforcement to follow someone's movements on the Internet. When smartphone owners surf the web, their movements can be tracked just as surely as their physical movements when they carry their cell phones from place to place. This type of tracking, which is done without the web surfer's permission, is commonly called digital shadowing.

Digital shadowing began as a way to tailor advertising to people's tastes. By keeping a record of the webpages that someone visits, an advertiser can determine which ads would be most likely to interest the person in the future. According to digital marketing research firm eMarketer, spending on online ads worldwide will likely reach $132 billion in 2015.

Most web surfers see nothing wrong with this practice, although they might find Internet ads annoying. However, privacy experts are concerned about digital shadowing. Many note that not only does it provide data about a person's personal preferences and habits, but sometimes this data also is combined with personal information culled from social media sites. Consequently, Sagi Leizerov of the accounting firm Ernst & Young's privacy services says, "It is a mistake to consider (online) tracking benign. It's both an opportunity for amazing connections of data, as well as a time bomb of revealing personal information you assume will be kept private."[33]

This personal information can be as seemingly harmless as what someone rates as being a "like" or a "dislike" on a site or preferences registered through an online instant poll. This information is often fed into tracking-data aggregators, websites or programs that collect related items of content to develop a profile of the web surfer.

In one of the other phones, within a text message and the iPhone's address book, there were fragments of information related to the owner's credit card number and PIN (personal identification number). Another smartphone held the name of the owner, the name of her bank, her passport number and its expiration date, her e-mail address, and the names and e-mail addresses of her contacts. Knowing a person's bank, experts say, is a key piece of information since it is then easy to impersonate a bank official via e-mail in order to gain information that might help a criminal access an account.

Moreover, Andy Jones, head of information security research at British Telecommunications, reports that with enough bits and pieces from a smartphone it is relatively easy to reconstruct a person's life,

Security experts who were asked to do forensic analysis of several cell phones found all kinds of personal information, including, in one instance, the user's passport number. Cell phones retain a large amount of information that could be used in problematic ways.

perhaps in order to build a legal or criminal case against him or her. According to Jones, "Out of context, an individual piece of information such as an SMS [short message service, or text message] is almost meaningless. But when you have a large volume of information—a person's diary for the year, his e-mails, the plans he's building—and you start to put them together, you can make some interesting discoveries."[36]

Privacy Concerns

The ACLU points out that these discoveries often include many personal details. The organization notes that

> the type of data stored on a smartphone can paint a near-complete picture of even the most private details of someone's personal life. Call history, voicemails, text messages and photographs can provide a catalogue of how—and with whom—a person spends his or her time, exposing everything from intimate photographs to 2 AM text messages. Web browsing history may include Google searches for Alcoholics Anonymous or local gay bars. Apps can expose what you're reading and listening to. Location information might uncover a visit to an abortion clinic, a political protest, or a psychiatrist.[37]

The ACLU is concerned that police have the right to search someone's mobile phone. This right is based on the fact that police are allowed to search the items in someone's possession if that person is being placed under arrest. However, the ACLU argues that when these laws were crafted, lawmakers never imagined the wealth of personal information that would one day be available in a smartphone. As the organization asserts,

> Before the age of smartphones, it was impossible for police to gather this much private information about a person's communications, historical movements, and private life during an

arrest. Our pockets and bags simply aren't big enough to carry paper records revealing that much data. We would have never carried around several years' worth of correspondence, for example—but today, five-year-old emails are just a few clicks away using the smartphone in your pocket.[38]

A case that illustrates the ACLU's concerns was heard by the US Supreme Court in April 2014. That case could decide whether the contents of a cell phone confiscated during an arrest can be examined by police without a warrant. Current law allows officers to search the pockets, wallet, or purse of a person who has been arrested. The issue before the court is whether a smartphone (which often contains a large amount of private information) can also be searched without a warrant.

The case in question involves college student David Riley, who was pulled over for expired car registration tags in 2009 in San Diego, California. When the police officer discovered that Riley's driver's license had expired as well, he searched the car and Riley's smartphone. In the car the officer found two loaded guns; on the smartphone the officer found photographs of gang members and a vehicle known to have been used in a drive-by shooting. This evidence ultimately led Riley to be convicted of attempted murder, for which he received a sentence of fifteen years to life. A decision in the Riley case, and another similar case, was expected later in the year.

Another concern is the fact that some police have accessed cell phone data secretly using scanning technology. In 2011 this practice came to light in Michigan, where state police were using a handheld mobile forensics device to obtain information from the cell phones of motorists stopped for minor traffic violations. The company offering the device, CelleBrite, claims that it can access existing, hidden, and deleted data from three thousand different types of phones, and a test of the device showed that it could acquire all photos and videos on an iPhone in less than two minutes. In complaining about Michigan's state police using this device at traffic stops, ACLU attorney Mark P. Fancher said,

> With certain exceptions that do not apply here, a search cannot occur without a warrant in which a judicial officer determines that there is probable cause to believe that the search

Selling Cell Phones

Someone who wants to sell a phone is typically advised to do a factory reset on the phone first. This is because a reset restores all of the phone's original settings, deletes all owner-added apps, and supposedly wipes all personal data. However, many security experts say enough data will remain on the phone to compromise the seller's safety and security. To prove this, security and identity theft expert Robert Siciliano bought and tested phones whose sellers thought they had been wiped clean of personal data. He found it relatively easy to retrieve the supposedly erased information, especially on phones with an Android operating system. He reports: "I found just about anything you can imagine someone would have in a digital format. I found family photos, personal documents, court documents, child support documents, user names and passwords, Social Security numbers and birthdates. I found employee records and tax documents. I also found a lot of pornography." Because of this, Siciliano advises people never to sell or donate their cell phones. Of his own he says, "I will take it and put it in a vice and I will drill holes through it. I will smash it with a sledgehammer. Or I'll put it in a bucket of salt water for a year. But you're not going to see me selling it."

Quoted in Herb Weisbaum, "Why You Should Never Sell Your Old Cell Phone," NBC News, May 8, 2012. http://business.nbcnews.com.

will yield evidence of criminal activity. A device that allows immediate, surreptitious intrusion into private data creates enormous risks that troopers will ignore these requirements to the detriment of the constitutional rights of persons whose cell phones are searched.[39]

Civil Suits

There is also the risk that personal information on a cell phone will be revealed as part of a civil lawsuit since many states allow phone records to be subpoenaed by a litigant in such a case. For example, in October

Infecting a SIM

According to some estimates, there are 7 billion modern SIM cards currently in circulation. Each one contains a chip that is essentially a small computer, with its own operating system, processor, and memory. Therefore, it is vulnerable in many of the same ways a computer is, and in 2013 German cryptographer Karsten Nohl discovered that SIMs can be infected with a virus. Moreover, this virus could enable hackers to commit payment-system fraud by accessing mobile payment apps and, with them, the phone owner's bank and credit card details.

Experts previously thought that SIMs were not susceptible to viruses, and they thought mobile payment apps were protected from invasion largely because of sandboxing. This feature shields payment apps, like Visa or PayPal, from one another and from anything else on the SIM card. (The term *sandboxing* comes from the metaphor that each app, by not interacting with the others, was playing in its own sandbox.) But Nohl developed a virus that can infect the SIM card in a cell phone remotely and break down sandbox protections, essentially because it gives the SIM's software a command it cannot handle, and in response the SIM abandons basic security checks and grants the virus full memory access to it. Consequently, Nohl says, "Give me any phone number and there is some chance I will, a few minutes later, be able to remotely control this SIM card and even make a copy of it." However, SIM card providers say they have not discovered any vulnerabilities in SIMs that would threaten the security of mobile payment apps.

Quoted in Parmy Olson, "SIM Cards Have Finally Been Hacked, and the Flaws Could Affect Millions of Phones," *Forbes*, July 21, 2013. www.forbes.com.

2013 a federal district court in California held that an employer could subpoena the personal cell phone records of a former employee while preparing to defend itself against the employee's claim that she was fired because of racial and sexual discrimination. The employer said it had instead fired the employee because she had been lying about her work hours and engaging in personal business on company time.

Records of all phone calls, text messages, and other data generated by her personal cell phone while she was supposed to be on the job would be directly relevant to this claim. The court therefore upheld the subpoena request, adding that an employee can have no expectations of privacy in regard to business-related records even if these records are associated with a personal cell phone.

Some states allow the subpoenaing of personal phone records unrelated to business as well. For example, Pennsylvania attorney Lisa Marie Vari says, "If you are contemplating divorce or in the midst of a divorce or custody battle you should know that your computer and cellular phone can be your best friend or your worst nightmare. Your spouse may be able to access your computer, e-mail, and cell phone records." She warns her clients that "records of incoming and outgoing calls from a cellular phone can be damaging information in a divorce or other family law case," and "a persistent spouse or opposing party can also seek to subpoena the text message records from a cellular company."[40] Vari suggests that her clients delete such information on their phones to make it harder for others to access it.

Thievery

Security experts say that deleting should also be used to make it harder for criminals to gain access to such information, although sometimes a phone owner might not realize just how much should be deleted in order to stay safe. Even something as seemingly minor as an entry on a phone's calendar can be a boon for thieves. Police report that there have been several cases in which a criminal spotted notations regarding a vacation or appointment on the calendar of a stolen phone and, using the owner's address (also found in the phone), planned a burglary of the person's home based on when he or she would be away.

Thieves have also mined information on a phone related to finances in order to steal money from its owner and/or commit identity theft. As Joe McGeehan of Toshiba's Telecommunications Research Laboratory notes, "If you've got all your personal information on there, like bank details, social security details and credit card information, then you're really asking for someone to 'become' you, or rob you, or invade your corporate life."[41] Since experts estimate that nearly 10 percent of Americans have had their cell phones stolen, phone owners need to consider whether they really want to have financial information stored in their phones.

Password Protection

Many people do not heed such warnings. According to a study released in January 2014 by the security software firm McAfee, nearly two-thirds of smartphone owners keep sensitive information on their mobile devices, including bank account information, passwords, and credit card numbers. In addition, roughly a fifth of Americans rarely or never delete any personal or intimate text messages, e-mails, or photos. Yet only about 40 percent have password protection on their devices, whereby the only people who can gain access to the phone must key in a password or pass code first.

"Sharing passwords with your partner might seem harmless, but it often puts you at risk for a 'revenge of the ex' situation, landing private information in a public platform for all to see."[42]

—Michelle Dennedy, chief privacy officer at McAfee.

Moreover, many of those who have password protection think nothing of sharing their password with a loved one, never imagining what could happen if the loved one becomes an enemy. Michelle Dennedy, chief privacy officer at McAfee, explains: "Sharing passwords with your partner might seem harmless, but it often puts you at risk for a 'revenge of the ex' situation, landing private information in a public platform for all to see. Everyone needs to be aware of the risks and take the steps to make sure their personal data is safe and secure."[42]

Keeping the Device Safe

Experts also warn that phones must be treated like wallets, kept close at hand to avoid their being stolen or lost. According to technology writer Sebastian Anthony, "When it comes to security, if a hacker has obtained physical access [to the phone], you've already lost."[43] Experienced hackers can quickly and easily break into a device. In 2013, for example, security researchers at the Georgia Institute of Technology created a hacking device masquerading as a phone charger that was able to break into a phone in under a minute. Their demonstration of this device exposed vulnerabilities within cell phone technology that gave many experts pause.

In an attempt to prevent a lost or stolen phone from having its information accessed, some smartphone manufacturers provide a security feature known as a kill switch, a way that an owner can shut down his or her phone remotely upon realizing it is missing. Some lawmakers have proposed making this feature mandatory as a way to protect consumers from theft. But a nonprofit organization representing cell phone carriers, CTIA-The Wireless Association (previously known as the Cellular Telecommunications Industry Association), says that kill switches come with a risk. Specifically, if hackers figure out how to control the feature, they could disable phones at will, including those used by police and government officials.

Another security feature is specific to iPhones that are pass code protected, so that a user must key in a number code into the phone in order to get it to work. In such cases, if someone keys in the wrong password ten times in a row, the phone will erase itself. However, a hacker has figured out how to bypass the password on a smartphone. To do this, he sends a text message to the phone that gets it to launch the web browser Internet Explorer and download and install software that then sends data from that phone to the hacker's phone. He has posted a video on how to do this on the website YouTube, along with another video on how text messages can be used to convince certain smartphones to stop encrypting their data.

Wiping Data

Because so much data can be gained from a device, experts warn people to erase, or wipe, information from their phones before discarding them. However, studies have shown that doing this is not as common a practice as it should be. During a study of 135 discarded cell phones, for example, security expert Andy Jones discovered that out of roughly 80 working cell phones and smartphones that he received from volunteers, cell phone recyclers, and online auctions, ten of the

Determined hackers can access smartphone data remotely. Smartphones are typically connected to the Internet whenever they are turned on, meaning hackers can break into them the same way they break into computers when users are online.

then Apple has patched only 70 of these holes. The remaining ones have apparently not been exploited, but experts warn that this might change someday.

Unsecure Networks

Experts also warn that apps can make a phone vulnerable to hackers regardless of the operating system. Many apps store data on the phone, and if this is done insecurely, an attacker using the same network, such as a public wi-fi network, can steal information being sent to and from the app, even if the device is an iPhone. Andy Swift, a mobile security researcher, explains that "such data can be easily extracted and may include . . . personal data. At the end of the day if not investigated, the end user has no idea what data the application is accessing and sending to a server somewhere."[46]

In reporting on this problem, technology writer Tom Brewster of the *Guardian* says, "All of these attacks could easily be executed on public or unprotected Wi-Fi networks, so you should be especially careful when using such services, refraining from sharing sensitive data over them. And they should avoid any untrusted networks."[47]

Unsecured, or open, wireless networks are unsafe because any and all information sent over such a network, which does not require the user to enter a security code, is available for anyone to intercept. This means that using an open network opens up a user's data to anyone else with access to that network, including a hacker. And this is true not just when it comes to apps. Using a web browser to visit Internet sites also poses risks. For example, if someone logs into his or her e-mail account while on an unsecured network, then a hacker can use that log-in information to access the e-mail account too, along with any personal information that might be in the account. This is the same risk that laptop users take when they use their devices to access the Internet on unsecured wireless networks.

> "At the end of the day if not investigated, the end user has no idea what data the application is accessing and sending to a server somewhere."[46]
>
> —*Andy Swift, mobile security researcher.*

Experts say that smartphones share another vulnerability with laptops as well. In 2013 several telecommunications companies confirmed technology experts' suspicions that hackers were making viruses targeted to cell phones. A virus is a type of malware that can replicate itself and spread to other devices, thereby providing new routes of malware infection. Smartphones were once thought immune to them.

Also in 2013, white-hat hackers—good hackers who engage in hacking as a way to expose security risks that might hurt people—announced that they had found a way to tap into Verizon cell phones using a device called a femtocell, or wireless network creator. This device was created to boost signals in rural areas with poor cell phone reception. However, the hackers figured out how to couple it with free software downloaded online in order to intercept information sent by an Internet browser, such as log-in and password information sent to a banking site.

Given such advances, experts say that cell phone owners can never assume that they will be as protected tomorrow as they are today. Therefore, it is necessary to develop good habits when it comes to cell phone security. These include keeping your phone in your possession as much as possible; not downloading anything into your smartphone unless it comes from a known, safe source; and thinking hard before storing sensitive information on your phone. In addition, the Internet Crime Complaint Center task force advises, "Use the same precautions on your mobile phone as you would on your computer when using the Internet."[48]

Photo Privacy and Safety Concerns

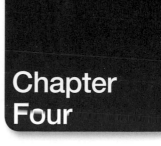

Chapter Four

In 2013 the British newspaper the *Sun* reported that the London flat, or apartment, of English actress/model Helen Flanagan had been burglarized. One of the items taken was her cell phone—and when she learned about the theft, her first concern was not her personal information but the photos stored on the phone. They were of a sexual nature, and Flanagan feared that someone would post them on the Internet. A friend told the *Sun*, "Helen's mortified at the thought of the photos and texts going on the web. She doesn't want her solo amateur stuff bouncing around the net for ever. It's all very well doing sexy poses for mags in a studio. But daring shots taken in the privacy of her home are very different and were never taken to be made public."[49]

Sexting

Because of the risk of phone theft, experts advise not storing sensitive photos on a cell phone or smartphone. They also recommend not sending sexually suggestive photos or messages to others, even loved ones. Nonetheless, according to the McAfee study released in January 2014, more than half of American adults have sent or received sexually explicit photos via their cell phones, a practice commonly known as sexting.

Sexting can be a threat to privacy and security because far too often the photos end up in the wrong hands. McAfee found that although 94 percent of Americans believe they can trust their partners not to share their revealing photos, 13 percent of adults have had their partners share these images without permission. Moreover, one in ten ex-partners have threatened to share the pictures with others after a breakup, and such threats are carried out 60 percent of the time. McAfee also reports that men get threatened more than women, and these threats are more often carried out.

Sharing can entail forwarding the photo in an e-mail, but more often it involves posting the photo on Internet sites. (In either case, if the subject of the photo is a minor, sharing the photo is illegal.) Once this occurs, strangers can easily appropriate the photo for their own uses. According to research conducted by the Internet Watch Foundation in 2012, 88 percent of self-made sexual photos posted on the Internet were subsequently copied from their original online location, such as a social networking site, to be viewed elsewhere. Many ended up on pornography sites.

Sneaking Photos

But not all sexted photos are self-made. Some are taken without the victim's knowledge. For example, there have been cases of teenage girls passing out drunk at a party only to find sexually suggestive pictures of themselves posted on the Internet the following day by other partygoers. Some of these cases have resulted in the victim committing suicide because of the teasing and embarrassment that came of having classmates see such pictures.

It is also possible for a stranger to take such a sexually suggestive picture remotely. This can be accomplished using malware that secretly turns on cameras. Whereas some of the people who sneak this malware on to a phone intend for it to provide information about the victim's private conversations via the camera's microphone, far more hope to capture naked images.

Joseph Steinberg, a columnist with *Forbes* magazine, reports that malware designed to activate cameras, snap secret pictures, and forward these pictures to a stranger has become highly sophisticated. This is evidenced by the fact that some versions can result in digital photos with realistic skin tones because they can analyze and adjust colors. He says that this should be a matter of great concern to cell phone owners. He elaborates:

> Considering the percentage of phone users who bring their phones into bedrooms, bathrooms, and other areas in which they usually do not want to be photographed, such malware could put nearly the entire adult population of the West-

Sexually suggestive photos and texts sent by cell phone often end up in the wrong hands. This can be especially harmful when it happens to teenagers who must endure constant teasing and sometimes harassment by classmates.

ern World at risk of serious embarrassment. Even without the flesh-tone analysis capability, smartphone malware that shares surreptitiously taken photographs clearly poses severe privacy risks.[50]

Permanence

Adding to victims' distress over such photos is the fact that these images are difficult to remove from the Internet once they are posted on a website. Lawyer Lori Andrews, director of the Institute for Science, Law, and Technology in Chicago, explains that under federal law, specifically the Communications Decency Act, Internet providers cannot be forced to take down content for invading a person's privacy or even defaming them. She says, "I could sue The New York Times for invading my privacy or Rolling Stone for defaming me. But I couldn't sue and get my picture off a website called slutty seventhgraders.com."[51]

"If five, ten copies of [an embarrassing] picture are out there [on the Internet], chances are I'm going to find it."[54]

—Larry Zillox, president of Investigative Research Specialists.

Moreover, an image shared via e-mail can continue circulating forever. As Jeffrey Rosen, a district attorney in Santa Clara County, California, notes in regard to cases where teenagers are embarrassed by sexted photos,

> What's really changed is that before the Internet you could do something really stupid and maybe someone would take a picture of it, so there's the picture and the film, and you could physically capture that. You can't capture things on the Internet. . . . [And] it's one thing that people are gossiping about you in school, but when you add images that they can keep forwarding, it really can seem like the whole world knows.[52]

Permanent Problems

In most cases, something posted online remains there forever. This is why, experts say, people must be very careful about what they post. The odds are that it will always be accessible. Nonetheless, the McAfee study found that about 15 percent of people who have had personal information and/or embarrassing photos shared online hired an attorney and took legal actions to have these things removed from the

A Dropbox Surprise

Dropbox is an app that provides users with a place to store copies of their documents, videos, and photos. When users copy these materials into a Dropbox file on their phone or computer, another copy is automatically stored in a corresponding Dropbox file on the Internet. Smartphones provide the option of having photos automatically stored on the Internet (also known as the cloud) as soon as the photos are taken via Dropbox's camera upload feature.

This was the case with the smartphone of a mother in Brooklyn, New York, and it resulted in a shocking discovery. A few weeks after her phone was stolen at a street fair, she was viewing her Dropbox materials when she spotted racy photos of an unknown couple. Unfortunately, the police were unwilling to help the woman identify the couple, saying there was no way to know if they were the ones who stole the phone or if they had simply bought the phone from the thief without knowing it was stolen or linked to Dropbox.

Internet. There are also companies that specialize in removing such content, but this service can be expensive.

Some people have found, though, that over time their embarrassing images disappear. This is because of the status of the website where they were posted. Larry Zillox, president of Investigative Research Specialists, explains: "Very often, places where pictures are posted on the Internet just go away. The company name gets sold, and the new owners just delete the old content. Sometimes they delete accounts if you haven't logged in in a while."[53]

However, when embarrassing photographs are posted in several places online, it is rare for all of them to disappear. As Zillox—who specializes in searching for photographs that will place a politician's opponents in a bad light—notes, "If you have patience and are willing to sift through a lot of stuff, some gems might still show up. . . . If five, ten copies of a picture are out there, chances are I'm going to find it."[54]

Screen Captures

Because of concerns about images remaining forever on the Internet, two Stanford University students, Evan Spiegel and Robert Murphy, released a photo-messaging application in September 2011 that they claim allows users to share photographs and videos without the images becoming permanent. Called Snapchat, this app lets users add text and drawings to their own photos and videos before sharing them with people on a list that the user controls. Users also set a limit as to how long their friends can view the images, known as Snaps; the typical time period is one to ten seconds. During this time, in order to keep viewing the image, recipients must keep a finger on the photo or video; after the time limit has expired, the recipients no longer see it. Snapchat then deletes the images from its servers.

The app called Snapchat allows users to control how long photos and videos can be viewed by friends. Typically, images are deleted from the app's server within ten seconds.

As of January 2014, Snapchat users had sent 400 million photos and videos each day, believing that none of these would be viewable once their sharing period was over. However, some experts in digital technology say that it is possible to view Snaps long after they have supposedly disappeared. For example, Richard Hickman of Decipher Forensics used forensics software to retrieve old Snaps that had been viewed on Android phones. (Hickman's work includes pulling evidence from phones to use in divorce cases and to help find missing persons.) Of his ability to retrieve Snaps, he says, "I was surprised no one else had done it because of how easy it was."[55]

It is also easy to use a screen shot to capture Snaps or any other photo or video viewed on a smartphone. A screen shot is a feature on a smartphone whereby the phone takes a picture of whatever is shown on its screen. Joseph Steinberg reports that "it is technologically impossible to guarantee that a recipient does not generate a screen capture, and even a warning to the sender of the recipient's attempts to do so . . . may be circumventable."[56]

Steinberg is concerned that Snapchat is giving a false sense of security to its users, encouraging them to engage in risky behavior. He says, "If people think that their private photos and videos can be shared in a manner that is truly self-destructing . . . they are more likely to send them to others." Steinberg believes that the idea of impermanence is especially likely to increase the amount of sexting, with possibly upsetting results for those who engage in it. He cautions, "The only way to ensure that a photo or video is not distributed is not to distribute it."[57]

> "The only way to ensure that a photo or video is not distributed is not to distribute it."[57]
>
> —Forbes columnist Joseph Steinberg.

Sensitive Areas

But embarrassing photos are not the only images to be problematic for the users of cell phone cameras. Seemingly innocuous images can sometimes get a camera user in trouble. For example, if a person pulls out a cell phone and takes a picture in an area where photography is restricted, such as a federal courthouse or gambling casino, that person will likely be confronted by security guards. Similarly, taking a photo in a doctor's waiting room could lead to a strongly worded request to delete the photo in order to protect patients' right to privacy.

Given the problems that taking a photograph in the wrong place can cause, Steinberg advises phone owners to take measures to prevent unintentional photography. He says that users should "ensure that the camera cannot take pictures when you do not want it to, by putting the phone in a case, bag, pocket, or drawer that covers the camera whenever it is not supposed to function. Alternatively, or as an additional line of defense, you can put a small piece of an opaque sticky-note over the camera."[58]

This practice will also help cell phone owners avoid becoming crime victims. Some thieves have been known to activate a camera remotely in order to study its surroundings for the purposes of a burglary. In this way, they can know where valuables are and how a targeted house is laid out. Cameras also have been activated remotely in order to attempt to photograph someone keying a password into a bank's automatic teller machine.

> "Ensure that the camera cannot take pictures when you do not want it to, by putting the phone in a case, bag, pocket, or drawer that covers the camera whenever it is not supposed to function."[58]
>
> —Forbes columnist Joseph Steinberg.

Photographing Numbers

Similarly, in 2013 researchers at the University of Cambridge developed a program that uses a smartphone's camera to learn someone's phone PIN. The program activates the phone's camera and films the person's face while he or she is using the keypad. These images allow the software to estimate the orientation of the phone based on where the person is looking and how the phone is being held, and it then combines this information with keypad-touch sounds being picked up by the phone's microphone in order to determine what numbers are being entered. (Many apps produce a vibration each time a number is keyed in, and this vibration can also be picked up by the phone microphone.)

One of the researchers, Ross Anderson, a professor of security engineering at Cambridge, explains the process: "We watch how your face appears to move as you jiggle your phone by typing. It did sur-

Legal Troubles

Many young people who engage in sexting do not realize that it is illegal to send or receive sexually suggestive photos of anyone who is a minor. This is true even if all parties involved in the sexting are minors. If caught, both sender and receiver can be charged with distributing or receiving child pornography, regardless of whether all parties involved in the incident were friends and the person depicted in the photograph willingly participated in the sexting. A conviction could result in jail time and the requirement that the convicted person register as a sex offender.

Some people believe that such consequences are too dire for cases where all parties involved are teens and no one was harmed by the sexting. As an example of such a case, in 2012 four teenage boys in California received nude pictures from girls in their high school and then shared these with each other and with friends. None of them realized this was illegal. In addition, someone they gave the photos to then shared them via Twitter. Under California law, the boys had to be charged with the crime of distributing child pornography.

prise us how well it worked."[59] The images and sounds are captured in just a few seconds and are transferred to a remote server where the program performs its calculations. This means that the phone's user is unaware of the activity.

Anderson reports that the software was successful in determining a four-digit number more than 50 percent of the time, but it typically took five repetitions of the number in order to do so. There was a 60 percent success rate for eight-digit numbers after ten repetitions. This success rate is a matter of concern for security experts since PINs not only unlock pass code–protected phones but also are used for financial apps, including ones tied to bank accounts.

Some experts in digital technology, however, think that it is unnecessary to worry about software developed by researchers seeking to show what thieves might be capable of. For example, Christina DesMarais of *PC World* magazine says, "These researchers get paid to do this stuff and they have vast resources at their fingertips. While they can prove phones are capable of doing these kinds of tricks, and even if doing so gives real criminals ideas, the average hacker can't pull off such shenanigans on his own."[60]

Geotagging

There are also disagreements over whether concerns regarding the safety of posting family pictures on the Internet are overblown. Many people engage in this activity and consider it harmless, but others fear that shared photos will provide predators and thieves with a way to track down the people shown in the photos. This issue gained a great deal of attention in 2013, after a related warning went viral on Facebook and other social media sites and via e-mail. (When a message goes viral, it means that it is being shared so often that its circulation through the Internet is extremely rapid.) Embedded within the message was a clip that had been posted on YouTube of a 2010 NBC Action News report about the dangers of cell phone cameras.

The news story explained that photos taken with a smartphone camera and either e-mailed or uploaded to Internet sites could help someone locate the individual in the photo against that person's wishes. This is possible because of geotagging, or geographical tagging, which is the storage of location-based metadata in a JPEG image. (JPEG, or Joint Photographic Experts Group, is the type of image format most commonly used for digital photos because it allows such photos to have millions of colors.) Specifically, the camera tags the image with the latitude and longitude of the place where the photo was taken, and this information is stored in the same digital file that holds the photo as part of its exchangeable image file (EXIF) format metadata. This is a standard format among digital devices that dictates how additional data may be stored with images.

The idea behind geotagging is that it helps the photographer remember where a photo was taken. Tagging can provide other types of

Many people post family pictures on the Internet. Some experts say this is risky while others consider it to be harmless.

metadata as well: the date the image was taken, the device it was taken on, and the camera settings used to take it. Most digital cameras do not come with the ability to tag; instead, the photographer must either add special tagging hardware to the camera or use computer software to add the tag after the photo is taken. However, smartphone cameras come equipped with this special hardware so they can add the tags automatically, using the GPS locator technology that also comes with the camera to determine where the picture was taken.

When an image is uploaded to a website, the tags go right along with it. Consequently, someone with software that allows them to view tags would be able to download the image and locate the place where the photo was taken. This poses dangers depending on who accesses the information. For example, a pedophile might use it to find out where a child lives.

However, certain websites have taken steps to prevent someone with malicious intent from using a geotag to track down a potential victim. For example, Facebook says that when someone downloads photos from its site, that person will not be able to see the photo's metadata. Similarly, Twitter removes the metadata from a photo when that photo is uploaded, which also makes it unavailable to anyone who might view the photo. Still, other sites are not this secure in regard to geotags. According to Brett M. Christensen, who investigated the viral warning about geotags for the website Hoax-Slayer, these include the social network Google+ and the photo-sharing site Flickr, both of which retain all metadata.

In addition, a photo that has been directly copied onto the photographer's website will include geotags unless the photographer has taken certain precautions. The most basic precaution is to turn off the phone's GPS feature so that the camera cannot know the phone's location when it is taking the picture. But if the photo has already been taken and tagged when the photographer realizes the tag should be removed, there is tag-editing software that can change or remove the tag. Alternatively, the photographer can save the photo to a different format that does not support the kind of metadata on the photo.

Oversharing

But even without geotags, some people worry about the safety of posting pictures on social media and photo-sharing sites, particularly when the photos are of children. Parents and grandparents wonder whether doing this might expose young people to sexual predators or others who mean to do them harm. To prevent this possibility, some sites have privacy settings that keep strangers from having access to the photos. There is also an app in development that will allow people sharing photos to encrypt a section of the photo so that the section, such as the part showing a child, can be viewed only by someone with a pass code. The blocked part of the photo would be grayed out.

But despite such attempts to safeguard images, experts say that people should always think carefully before sharing any image with others. This is because once images are shared, they cannot be unshared, and there will always be a risk that hackers will find a way around any safeguards—and will perhaps also use the images to cause problems for those depicted in them.

> "You [do not] have to hand over your personal privacy to be part of the 21st century."[61]
>
> —Kevin Bankston, a lawyer at the Electronic Frontier Foundation.

Experts also say that while it is hard to maintain privacy and security when using cell phones, there is no reason to throw them away willingly. Or, as Kevin Bankston, a lawyer at the Electronic Frontier Foundation who specializes in privacy, points out, although cell phones might be integral to modern society, "you [do not] have to hand over your personal privacy to be part of the 21st century."[61]

Source Notes

Introduction: Benefits Versus Risks

1. *Consumer Reports*, "Keep Your Phone Safe," June 2013. http://consumerreports.org.

2. Quoted in Dan Bewley, "Experts Give Tips to Tulsans to Keep Phone from Being Hacked," News on 6, January 10, 2014. www.newson6.com.

3. Quoted in *Consumer Reports*, "Keep Your Phone Safe."

Chapter One: Keeping Conversations Private

4. Quoted in NBC News, "'Loveint': NSA Letter Discloses Employee Eavesdropping on Girlfriends, Spouses," September 26, 2013. www.nbcnews.com.

5. Shouse California Law Group, "Wiretapping & California Criminal Law: California Penal Code 631 PC." www.shouselaw.com.

6. Quoted in Glenn Greenwald, "Are All Telephone Calls Recorded and Accessible to the US Government?," *Guardian*, May 4, 2013. www.theguardian.com.

7. Quoted in Greenwald, "Are All Telephone Calls Recorded and Accessible to the US Government?"

8. American Civil Liberties Union, "Reform the Patriot Act: Section 215." www.aclu.org.

9. Quoted in Eileen Sullivan, "Obama Says Spying Not Abused, Will Continue," Associated Press, August 9, 2013. http://bigstory.ap.org.

10. Privacy Rights Clearing House, "Fact Sheet 9: Wiretapping and Eavesdropping on Telephone Calls." www.privacyrights.org.

11. Shouse California Law Group, "Wiretapping & California Criminal Law."

12. Digital Media Law Project, "Recording Phone Calls and Conversations." www.dmlp.org.

13. Joshua Sherman, "How to Turn Your Smartphone into a Spy Camera or Baby Monitor," *Digital Trends*, October 5, 2013. www.digitaltrends.com.

14. Quoted in Kieran Campbell, "Secret Phone Apps Used to Spy on Spouses," 9 News, November 29, 2013. http://news.ninemsn.com.au.

15. Quoted in Campbell, "Secret Phone Apps Used to Spy on Spouses."

16. FlexiSpy, "Spy on Mobiles, Cellphones, and Tablets." www.flexispy.com.

17. FlexiSpy, "Spy on Mobiles, Cellphones, and Tablets."

Chapter Two: Is Someone Tracking Your Movements?

18. Ben Goldacre, "How I Stalked My Girlfriend," *Family Abuse Center Blog*, September 14, 2013. www.familyabusecenter.org.

19. Quoted in Noam Cohen, "It's Tracking Your Every Move and You May Not Even Know," *New York Times*, March 26, 2011. www.nytimes.com.

20. Quoted in Lisa Fletcher and Cole Kazdin, "Cell Phone Spying Nightmare: 'You're Never the Same,'" ABC News, March 8, 2010. http://abcnews.go.com.

21. Quoted in Fletcher and Kazdin, "Cell Phone Spying Nightmare."

22. Quoted in Fletcher and Kazdin, "Cell Phone Spying Nightmare."

23. Quoted in Fletcher and Kazdin, "Cell Phone Spying Nightmare."

24. Quoted in News 10 Staff, KXTV, "Stalkers Turn to Cheap Cell Phone Spyware to Track Victims." www.news10.net.

25. Quoted in Cohen, "It's Tracking Your Every Move and You May Not Even Know."

26. Quoted in Cohen, "It's Tracking Your Every Move and You May Not Even Know."

27. Quoted in Jacob Gershman, "High Court in Massachusetts Rules Cell-Phone Data Requires Warrant," *Law Blog*, February 18, 2014. http://blogs.wsj.com.

28. Quoted in Jacob Gershman, "Appeals Court: No Warrant Needed for Phone Location Data," *Law Blog*, July 30, 2013. http://blogs.wsj.com.

29. Timothy B. Lee, "Documents Show Cops Making Up the Rules on Mobile Surveillance," Ars Technica, April 3, 2012. http://arstechnica.com.

30. Quoted in Eric Lichtblau, "Police Are Using Phone Tracking as a Routine Tool," *New York Times*, March 31, 2012. www.nytimes.com.

31. Lichtblau, "Police Are Using Phone Tracking as a Routine Tool."

32. Quoted in Lichtblau, "Police Are Using Phone Tracking as a Routine Tool."

33. Quoted in Byron Achohido, "Web Tracking Has Become a Privacy Time Bomb," *USA Today*, August 4, 2011. http://usatoday30.usatoday.com.

34. Quoted in Achohido, "Web Has Become a Privacy Time Bomb."

35. Quoted in Achohido, "Web Has Become a Privacy Time Bomb."

Chapter Three: Keeping Your Records Safe

36. Quoted in Linda Geddes, "Forensic Mobile Phone Work Reveals Threat to All of Us," *Computer Weekly*, October 2009. www.computerweekly.com.

37. Quoted in Mike Masnick, "The Details of What Information the Police Can Suck Out of Your Phone," TechDirt.com, March 1, 2013. www.techdirt.com.

38. Quoted in Masnick, "The Details of What Information the Police Can Suck Out of Your Phone."

39. Quoted in Paul Joseph Watson, "Cops Use Mobile Scanner to Steal Cellphone Data from Innocent Americans," InfoWars.com, April 20, 2011. www.infowars.com.

40. Lisa Marie Vari, "A Warning About Cell Phones & Text Messages," Lisa Marie Vari & Associates, PC. www.pafamilylawyers.com.

41. Quoted in Geddes, "Forensic Mobile Phone Work Reveals Threat to All of Us."

42. Quoted in McAfee, "Lovers Beware: Scorned Exes May Share Intimate Data and Images Online," press release, February 4, 2014. www.mcafee.com.

43. Sebastian Anthony, "Black Hat Hackers Break Into any iPhone in Under a Minute, Using a Malicious Charger," ExtremeTech, June 3, 2013. www.extremetech.com.

44. Quoted in Geddes, "Forensic Mobile Phone Work Reveals Threat to All of Us."

45. Quoted in Geddes, "Forensic Mobile Phone Work Reveals Threat to All of Us."

46. Quoted in Tom Brewster, "Feeling Smug That Your iPhone Can't Be Hacked? Not So Fast," Guardian, February 12, 2014. www.theguardian.com.

47. Brewster, "Feeling Smug That Your iPhone Can't Be Hacked?"

48. Quoted in Dara Kerr, "FBI Warns Users of Mobile Malware," CNET, October 15, 2012. http://news.cnet.com.

Chapter Four: Photo Privacy and Safety Concerns

49. Quoted in Stephen Moyes, "Helen in Terror as Sexy Pics Stolen," Sun, July 8, 2013. www.thesun.co.uk.

50. Joseph Steinberg, "Your Smartphone Can Photograph You, and Share Your Pictures, Without Your Knowledge," Forbes, June 4, 2013. www.forbes.com.

51. Quoted in Nina Burleigh, "Sexting, Shame, and Suicide," *Rolling Stone*, September 17, 2013. www.rollingstone.com.

52. Quoted in Burleigh, "Sexting, Shame, and Suicide."

53. Quoted in Patrick Di Justo, "Naked on the Internet Is Not Forever," *Atlantic*, February 2014. www.theatlantic.com.

54. Quoted in Di Justo, "Naked on the Internet Is Not Forever."

55. Quoted in Kashmire Hill, "Snapchats Don't Disappear: Forensics Firm Has Pulled Dozens of Supposedly-Deleted Photos from Android Phones," *Forbes*, May 9, 2013. www.forbes.com.

56. Joseph Steinberg, "Warning About SnapChat, Teenagers, and Online Photo Sharing," *Forbes*, February 11, 2013. www.forbes.com.

57. Steinberg, "Warning About SnapChat, Teenagers, and Online Photo Sharing."

58. Steinberg, "Your Smartphone Can Photograph You, and Share Your Pictures, Without Your Knowledge."

59. Quoted in BBC News, "Smartphone Pin Revealed by Camera and Microphone," November 11, 2013. www.bbc.co.uk.

60. Quoted in Sarah Jaffe, "How the Camera on Your Cell Phone Can Be Captured and Used to Spy on You," AlterNet, October 3, 2012. www.alternet.org.

61. Quoted in Cohen, "It's Tracking Your Every Move and You May Not Even Know."

American Civil Liberties Union (ACLU)
125 Broad St., 18th Floor
New York, NY 10004
phone: (212) 549-2500
website: www.aclu.org

The ACLU works to protect the rights and liberties established by the US Constitution and US laws, including the right to privacy.

CTIA-The Wireless Association
1400 Sixteenth St. NW, Suite 600
Washington, DC 20036
phone: (202) 736-3200
website: www.ctia.org

Previously known as the Cellular Telecommunications Industry Association, this international nonprofit membership organization supports the wireless communications industry and provides information on cell phone–related issues and laws.

Internet Crime Complaint Center (IC3)
website: www.ic3.gov

Established by the FBI and the National White Collar Crime Center, this agency receives Internet-related criminal complaints and refers them to the appropriate agencies for investigation. These complaints include crimes associated with smartphone access to the Internet.

Internet Watch Foundation

First Floor Building 7300, Suite 7310
Cambridge Research Park
Waterbeach, Cambridgeshire CB25 9TN
UK
phone: +44 1223 20 30 30
website: www.iwf.org.uk

This organization is dedicated to eliminating child sexual abuse images online, including those associated with sexting.

National Security Agency (NSA)

website: www.nsa.gov

Primarily concentrating on cryptography and the collection and dissemination of intelligence information, the NSA is a US defense agency that works to protect the nation and prevent domestic terrorist attacks.

Privacy International

62 Britton St.
London EC1M 5UY
UK
phone: +44 20 3422 4321
e-mail: info@privacy.org
website: www.privacyinternational.org

Privacy International is dedicated to fighting for the right to privacy not only in the United Kingdom but also elsewhere in the world. To this end, it also works to expose government surveillance efforts.

Privacy Rights Clearinghouse
3108 Fifth Ave., Suite A
San Diego, CA 92103
phone: (619) 298-3396
website: www.privacyrights.org

A nonprofit organization, Privacy Rights Clearinghouse is dedicated to educating individuals on privacy rights and issues and empowering them to protect their privacy. It also documents consumer complaints related to privacy, including those involving cell phone use, and works to help resolve these complaints.

For Further Research

Books

Dale-Marie Bryan, *Smartphone Safety and Privacy*. New York: Rosen, 2013.

Brian X. Chen, *Always On: How the iPhone Unlocked the Anything-Anytime-Anywhere Future—and Locked Us In*. Cambridge, MA: Da Capo, 2011.

Ronald J. Diebert, *Black Code: Surveillance, Privacy, and the Dark Side of the Internet*. Toronto: McClelland & Stewart, 2013.

Richard Guerry, *Public and Permanent: The Golden Rule of the 21st Century; Straight Talk About Digital Safety; The Real Consequences of Digital Abuse*. Bloomington, IN: Balboa Press, 2011.

Sheran Gunasekera, *Android Apps Security*. New York: Springer Science+Business Media, 2012.

Richard Hantula, *How Do Cell Phones Work?* New York: Chelsea Clubhouse, 2009.

Daniel V. Hoffman, *Blackjacking: Security Threats to BlackBerry Devices, PDAs, and Cell Phones in the Enterprise*. Indianapolis: Wiley, 2007.

Anmol Misra, *Android Security: Attacks and Defenses*. Boca Raton, FL: CRC, 2013.

Kevin D. Murray, *Is My Cell Phone Bugged?* Austin, TX: Emerald, 2011.

Theresa M. Payton and Ted Claypoole, *Privacy in the Age of Big Data: Recognizing Threats, Defending Your Rights, and Protecting Your Family*. Lanham, MD: Rowman & Littlefield, 2014.

Elizabeth Woyke, *The Smartphone: Anatomy of an Industry*. New York: New Press, 2014.

Index

tracking suspect's car with GPS, 33–35
    See also GPS (global positioning system)
Privacy International, 29
Privacy Rights Clearing House, 18
probable cause, 12

radio signals, 25
remote operations
    activation of cell phone cameras,
        52–53, 58
    data deletion, 7
    data retrieving, 46–47
Riley, David, 40
Romero, Anthony, 11
Rosen, Jeffrey, 54
roving bug, 18
Russell, Katherine, 14–15

sales of cell phones, 41
sandboxing, 42
scanning technology, 40–41
screen captures/shots, 57
screen locks, 7
sexting, 51–52, 59
Sherman, Joshua, 21
Shouse California Law Group, 12, 19
Siciliano, Robert, 28–29, 41
SIM (subscriber identity module) cards,
    21–22, 37, 42
smartphones
    location tracking and, 26, 26–27, 61
    number of Americans using, 7
    as small computer, 7
Snapchat, 56, 56–57
Snowden, Edward, 20
Spiegel, Evan, 56
Spitz, Malte, 31
spoofing, 47
Sports Tracker, 37
spy SIM card readers, 21
spyware/snoopware, 22, 23, 47
stalkers/stalking
    apps installed for other purposes used
        by, 8, 27, 37
    described, 27–30
    ease of, 24
    geotagging, 60–62
    listening to phone conversations,
        28–29

See also GPS (global positioning
    system)
Steinberg, Joseph, 52–53, 57, 58
Stingray tracking, 33
stolen phones, hacking, 44–45
subpoenas, 32
subscriber identity module (SIM) cards,
    21–22, 37, 42
Sun (British newspaper), 51
Supreme Court GPS decision, 33–35
surveillance by government. *See*
    government surveillance
surveillance by individuals
    devices available for, 18–19, **19**,
        21–22
    hacking as data is transmitted, 22
    reasons for, 22–23
    spyware/snoopware for, 22
    stolen phones and, 10
    See also GPS (global positioning
        system); stalkers/stalking
Swift, Andy, 49
Symantec, 47

terrorism and surveillance. *See* National
    Security Agency (NSA) metadata
    collection program
text messages, 14
theft
    banking passwords, 6
    credit card information, 6
    of information from mobile payment
        apps, 42
    personal data to aid, 43–44
    of phones to gather information, 44
tracking. *See* data tracking; location
    tracking
Twitter, 62

unsecure networks, 7, 48–50
USA Patriot Act, Section 14, 14
USA Today (newspaper), 33

Vari, Lisa Marie, 43
Verizon wiretapping fee, 17
videos. *See* photos
viruses, 42, 49–50
Virzi, Adam, 22–23

77

Patricia D. Netzley has written dozens of books for children, teens, and adults. A member of the Society of Children's Book Writers and Illustrators, she has also worked as an editor and a writing instructor.